50 Snack Recipes for Home

By: Kelly Johnson

Table of Contents

- Guacamole with Tortilla Chips
- Hummus and Veggie Sticks
- Caprese Skewers
- Deviled Eggs
- Popcorn with Parmesan and Rosemary
- Fruit Salad Cups
- Antipasto Platter
- Spinach and Artichoke Dip
- Mini BLT Sandwiches
- Greek Yogurt Parfait
- Stuffed Jalapeños
- Cucumber Slices with Cream Cheese
- Buffalo Cauliflower Bites
- Baked Sweet Potato Fries
- Bruschetta on Toasted Baguette
- Cheese and Crackers Platter
- Edamame with Sea Salt
- Mini Quesadillas
- Trail Mix with Nuts and Dried Fruits
- Smoked Salmon Crostini
- Baked Zucchini Chips
- Chicken Satay Skewers
- Sliced Apple with Peanut Butter
- Mini Meatballs with Dipping Sauce
- Rice Cake with Avocado and Radish
- Chocolate-Dipped Strawberries
- Stuffed Mushrooms
- Pita Bread with Tzatziki
- Greek Spanakopita Triangles
- Roasted Chickpeas
- Shrimp Cocktail
- Brussel Sprout Chips
- Mini Tacos with Guacamole
- Mango Salsa with Tortilla Chips
- Crab Rangoon

- Cherry Tomato and Mozzarella Bites
- Artisanal Cheese Plate
- Teriyaki Chicken Skewers
- Nut Butter Energy Bites
- Avocado Egg Rolls
- Beet Chips
- Raspberry Almond Brie Bites
- Baked Buffalo Wings
- Cottage Cheese and Pineapple Cups
- Stuffed Dates with Goat Cheese
- Pretzel Bites with Mustard Dip
- Chocolate Almond Clusters
- Smashed Avocado Toast
- Lemon Garlic Roasted Chickpeas
- Pimento Cheese Stuffed Celery

Guacamole with Tortilla Chips

Guacamole:

Ingredients:

- 3 ripe avocados
- 1 small red onion, finely diced
- 2 tomatoes, diced
- 1/4 cup fresh cilantro, chopped
- 1-2 cloves garlic, minced
- Juice of 2 limes
- Salt and pepper to taste
- Optional: Jalapeño, diced (for some heat)

Instructions:

Cut the avocados in half, remove the pits, and scoop the flesh into a mixing bowl.
Mash the avocados with a fork or potato masher until you reach your desired level of smoothness.
Add the diced red onion, tomatoes, cilantro, minced garlic, and optional diced jalapeño to the mashed avocados.
Squeeze the juice of two limes into the bowl, and season with salt and pepper to taste.
Gently mix all the ingredients together until well combined.
Taste and adjust the lime, salt, and pepper levels according to your preference.
Optional: Garnish with additional cilantro or a slice of lime.

Tortilla Chips:

- Purchase your favorite store-bought tortilla chips, or make your own by cutting corn tortillas into triangles and baking or frying them until crispy.

Serving:

- Serve the freshly made guacamole with the tortilla chips on the side for dipping.

Enjoy the creamy texture of the guacamole, the freshness of the tomatoes and cilantro, and the crunch of the tortilla chips. Guacamole with tortilla chips is perfect for parties, gatherings, or a tasty snack any time of the day.

Hummus and Veggie Sticks

Hummus:

Ingredients:

- 1 can (15 ounces) chickpeas, drained and rinsed
- 1/4 cup tahini (sesame paste)
- 1/4 cup extra-virgin olive oil, plus more for drizzling
- 2 tablespoons fresh lemon juice
- 2 cloves garlic, minced
- 1 teaspoon ground cumin
- Salt and black pepper to taste
- Water (as needed for desired consistency)

Instructions:

In a food processor, combine the chickpeas, tahini, olive oil, lemon juice, minced garlic, cumin, salt, and black pepper.
Blend until the mixture is smooth and creamy. If the hummus is too thick, add water, one tablespoon at a time, until you achieve your desired consistency.
Taste the hummus and adjust the seasoning as needed, adding more salt, pepper, or lemon juice.
Once the hummus is ready, transfer it to a serving bowl.
Drizzle with olive oil and garnish with a sprinkle of cumin or paprika if desired.

Veggie Sticks:

Ingredients:

- Carrot sticks
- Cucumber slices
- Bell pepper strips (assorted colors)
- Celery sticks

Instructions:

Wash and peel the carrots, if desired. Cut them into sticks.
Wash and slice the cucumber into rounds or sticks.
Wash and cut the bell peppers into strips.
Wash and cut the celery into sticks.

Serving:

- Arrange the hummus and veggie sticks on a platter or individual plates.
- Serve the hummus with the veggie sticks for dipping.
- Enjoy the combination of creamy hummus and crisp, fresh vegetables.

Hummus and veggie sticks are not only tasty but also a great source of fiber, vitamins, and minerals. This snack is perfect for parties, picnics, or a healthy treat any time you're craving a satisfying and nutritious option.

Caprese Skewers

Caprese Skewers:

Ingredients:

- Cherry or grape tomatoes
- Fresh mozzarella balls (bocconcini)
- Fresh basil leaves
- Balsamic glaze (store-bought or homemade)
- Wooden or bamboo skewers

Instructions:

Prepare Ingredients:
- Wash the cherry or grape tomatoes and pat them dry.
- Drain any liquid from the fresh mozzarella balls.
- Wash and dry the fresh basil leaves.

Assemble Skewers:
- Thread a tomato onto the skewer, followed by a mozzarella ball and a fresh basil leaf.
- Repeat the pattern until the skewer is filled, leaving a small space at the top for easy handling.

Arrange on Platter:
- Arrange the assembled Caprese skewers on a serving platter.

Drizzle with Balsamic Glaze:
- Just before serving, drizzle the Caprese skewers with balsamic glaze.

Serve:
- Serve the Caprese skewers immediately as a refreshing and flavorful appetizer.

Balsamic Glaze (Optional):

Ingredients:

- 1 cup balsamic vinegar
- 2 tablespoons honey or brown sugar (optional, for sweetness)

Instructions:

Combine Ingredients:

- In a small saucepan, combine balsamic vinegar and honey or brown sugar (if using).

Simmer:
- Bring the mixture to a simmer over medium heat.

Reduce and Thicken:
- Reduce the heat to low and simmer for 10-15 minutes or until the balsamic vinegar has thickened to your desired consistency. It should coat the back of a spoon.

Cool:
- Allow the balsamic glaze to cool before using.

Drizzle:
- Drizzle the cooled balsamic glaze over the Caprese skewers just before serving.

Caprese skewers are not only visually appealing but also burst with the flavors of fresh tomatoes, creamy mozzarella, and aromatic basil. They make an excellent appetizer for parties, gatherings, or any occasion where you want to showcase simple and delicious ingredients.

Deviled Eggs

Ingredients:

- 6 large eggs
- 2 tablespoons mayonnaise
- 1 teaspoon Dijon mustard
- 1 teaspoon white vinegar
- Salt and black pepper to taste
- Paprika, for garnish
- Chopped fresh chives or parsley, for garnish (optional)

Instructions:

Boil the Eggs:
- Place the eggs in a single layer in a saucepan and cover with water. Bring the water to a boil, then reduce the heat to a simmer. Cook the eggs for 10-12 minutes.

Cool and Peel:
- Once cooked, transfer the eggs to an ice water bath to cool. Once cooled, peel the eggs.

Slice and Remove Yolks:
- Cut the hard-boiled eggs in half lengthwise. Carefully remove the yolks and place them in a mixing bowl.

Prepare Filling:
- Mash the egg yolks with a fork. Add mayonnaise, Dijon mustard, white vinegar, salt, and black pepper. Mix until smooth and well combined.

Fill the Egg Whites:
- Spoon or pipe the yolk mixture back into the egg whites, creating a smooth and even filling.

Garnish:
- Sprinkle paprika over the filled eggs for a classic touch. You can also garnish with chopped fresh chives or parsley if desired.

Chill:
- Refrigerate the deviled eggs for at least 30 minutes before serving to allow the flavors to meld and the filling to set.

Serve:
- Arrange the deviled eggs on a serving platter and serve chilled.

Deviled eggs are a versatile appetizer, and you can customize the filling with additional ingredients like finely chopped pickles, relish, or a dash of hot sauce for a spicy kick. They are perfect for potlucks, picnics, or any gathering where you want to offer a classic and tasty finger food.

Popcorn with Parmesan and Rosemary

Ingredients:

- 1/2 cup popcorn kernels
- 2 tablespoons olive oil
- 1/3 cup grated Parmesan cheese
- 2 tablespoons fresh rosemary, finely chopped
- Salt to taste
- Black pepper to taste

Instructions:

Pop the Popcorn:
- Heat the olive oil in a large pot with a tight-fitting lid over medium heat. Add a few popcorn kernels to the pot and cover it. Once the test kernels pop, add the remaining popcorn kernels, cover, and shake the pot to coat the kernels with oil.

Pop the Corn:
- Continue shaking the pot occasionally to ensure even popping. When the popping slows down, remove the pot from heat.

Season the Popcorn:
- In a separate bowl, mix the freshly popped popcorn with grated Parmesan cheese and finely chopped fresh rosemary. Toss the popcorn until evenly coated.

Season with Salt and Pepper:
- Season the popcorn with salt and black pepper to taste. Toss again to distribute the seasonings.

Serve:
- Transfer the Popcorn with Parmesan and Rosemary to a serving bowl or individual containers.

Enjoy:
- Enjoy the savory and aromatic popcorn as a delicious snack.

Tips:

- Make sure to use fresh rosemary for the best flavor.
- Adjust the amount of Parmesan, rosemary, salt, and pepper according to your taste preferences.

This Popcorn with Parmesan and Rosemary is a perfect blend of cheesy, herby, and savory flavors. It's an excellent choice for movie nights, parties, or any time you're in the mood for a gourmet popcorn experience.

Fruit Salad Cups

Ingredients:

- 1 cup watermelon, diced
- 1 cup pineapple, diced
- 1 cup grapes, halved
- 1 cup strawberries, hulled and quartered
- 1 cup kiwi, peeled and diced
- 1 cup blueberries
- 1-2 tablespoons honey or maple syrup (optional, for sweetness)
- Fresh mint leaves for garnish (optional)

Instructions:

Prepare the Fruits:
- Wash and prepare all the fruits. Dice the watermelon, pineapple, kiwi, and strawberries. Halve the grapes.

Combine Fruits:
- In a large bowl, combine all the prepared fruits, including blueberries. Gently toss them together to mix.

Optional Sweetener:
- If desired, drizzle honey or maple syrup over the fruit salad to add a touch of sweetness. Toss again to coat the fruits evenly.

Chill:
- Refrigerate the fruit salad for at least 30 minutes to allow the flavors to meld and the salad to chill.

Serve in Cups:
- Spoon the chilled fruit salad into individual cups or bowls.

Garnish:
- Garnish the fruit salad cups with fresh mint leaves for a burst of aroma and added freshness.

Enjoy:
- Serve the Fruit Salad Cups chilled and enjoy this vibrant and healthy treat.

Tips:

- Feel free to customize the fruit selection based on your preferences and seasonal availability.
- Squeeze a bit of fresh lime or lemon juice over the fruit salad for a citrusy twist.

Fruit Salad Cups are not only delicious but also a great way to incorporate a variety of vitamins and antioxidants into your diet. They are perfect for brunches, picnics, or as a light and refreshing snack on a warm day.

Antipasto Platter

Ingredients:

- Assorted cured meats (e.g., prosciutto, salami, coppa)
- Various cheeses (e.g., mozzarella, provolone, Parmesan)
- Olives (green and black varieties)
- Marinated artichoke hearts
- Roasted red peppers
- Cherry tomatoes
- Fresh figs or dried fruits
- Grilled or pickled vegetables (e.g., eggplant, zucchini, bell peppers)
- Breadsticks or grissini
- Bread or crackers
- Olive oil for drizzling
- Balsamic glaze (optional)
- Fresh herbs for garnish (e.g., basil, rosemary)

Instructions:

Arrange the Meats and Cheeses:
- Start by placing a variety of cured meats and cheeses on the platter. Fold or roll the meats for an attractive presentation.

Add Olives and Pickled Items:
- Arrange olives, marinated artichoke hearts, and any other pickled items on the platter. This adds tanginess and depth to the flavors.

Include Roasted Vegetables:
- Position roasted red peppers, grilled vegetables, or any roasted components on the platter for a smoky and savory touch.

Incorporate Fresh Fruits:
- Add fresh fruits like cherry tomatoes and figs for a burst of sweetness that complements the savory elements.

Place Bread and Crackers:
- Arrange breadsticks, grissini, or slices of crusty bread around the platter. Include crackers for variety.

Drizzle with Olive Oil:
- Drizzle a good-quality olive oil over the meats, cheeses, and vegetables for richness and flavor.

Optional Balsamic Glaze:
- Optionally, drizzle balsamic glaze over certain components for added sweetness and depth.

Garnish with Fresh Herbs:

- Garnish the platter with fresh herbs such as basil or rosemary for a touch of brightness.

Serve:
- Serve the Antipasto Platter at room temperature and let your guests enjoy the variety of flavors.

Tips:

- Customize the platter based on your preferences and seasonal availability.
- Consider the preferences and dietary restrictions of your guests when selecting ingredients.

An Antipasto Platter is a versatile and visually appealing option for entertaining. It's perfect for gatherings, parties, or as a light and satisfying appetizer before a meal.

Spinach and Artichoke Dip

Ingredients:

- 1 (10-ounce) package frozen chopped spinach, thawed and drained
- 1 (14-ounce) can artichoke hearts, drained and chopped
- 1/2 cup mayonnaise
- 1/2 cup sour cream
- 1 cup grated Parmesan cheese
- 1 cup shredded mozzarella cheese
- 1 teaspoon minced garlic
- 1/2 teaspoon onion powder
- Salt and black pepper to taste
- 1/4 teaspoon red pepper flakes (optional, for heat)
- Tortilla chips, bread, or fresh vegetables for dipping

Instructions:

Preheat the Oven:
- Preheat your oven to 375°F (190°C).

Prepare Spinach and Artichokes:
- Thaw the frozen chopped spinach and squeeze out any excess water. Chop the drained artichoke hearts.

Mix Ingredients:
- In a large mixing bowl, combine the chopped spinach, chopped artichokes, mayonnaise, sour cream, grated Parmesan cheese, shredded mozzarella cheese, minced garlic, onion powder, salt, black pepper, and red pepper flakes (if using). Mix well until all ingredients are evenly combined.

Transfer to Baking Dish:
- Transfer the mixture to a baking dish, spreading it evenly.

Bake:
- Bake in the preheated oven for about 25-30 minutes or until the dip is hot and bubbly, and the top is golden brown.

Broil (Optional):
- If you prefer a more golden and bubbly top, you can broil the dip for an additional 2-3 minutes, keeping a close eye to prevent burning.

Serve:
- Remove from the oven and let it cool for a few minutes. Serve the Spinach and Artichoke Dip with tortilla chips, bread, or fresh vegetables for dipping.

Tips:

- Adjust the seasonings according to your taste preference.
- You can use fresh spinach instead of frozen. Simply blanch it, chop, and squeeze out excess water.

Spinach and Artichoke Dip is a crowd-pleaser and a classic party favorite. It's a comforting and indulgent appetizer that's sure to be a hit at any gathering.

Mini BLT Sandwiches

Ingredients:

- Mini dinner rolls or slider buns
- Bacon strips, cooked crispy
- Cherry or grape tomatoes, sliced
- Fresh lettuce leaves (e.g., iceberg or Romaine)
- Mayonnaise
- Toothpicks or small skewers

Instructions:

Prepare the Ingredients:
- Cook bacon until crispy. Slice cherry or grape tomatoes into thin rounds. Wash and dry the lettuce leaves.

Slice the Rolls:
- If the mini dinner rolls or slider buns are not pre-sliced, carefully slice them in half horizontally.

Assemble the Mini BLTs:
- Spread a small amount of mayonnaise on the bottom half of each roll.
- Place a lettuce leaf on the bottom half of the roll.
- Add a slice of tomato on top of the lettuce.
- Break a crispy bacon strip in half and arrange the halves on top of the tomato.
- Top with the other half of the roll.

Secure with Toothpicks:
- Secure each Mini BLT with a toothpick or small skewer to hold the layers together.

Serve:
- Arrange the Mini BLT Sandwiches on a serving platter and serve immediately.

Tips:

- Customize the sandwiches by adding a smear of mustard or a slice of cheese.
- For a variation, consider adding a small slice of avocado or a dollop of guacamole.

These Mini BLT Sandwiches are not only delicious but also visually appealing, making them a perfect addition to cocktail parties, brunches, or any event where you want to serve tasty and bite-sized treats.

Greek Yogurt Parfait

Ingredients:

- 1 cup Greek yogurt (plain or flavored)
- 1/2 cup granola
- 1/2 cup fresh berries (e.g., strawberries, blueberries, raspberries)
- 1 tablespoon honey or maple syrup (optional)
- Nuts or seeds for topping (e.g., sliced almonds, chia seeds)

Instructions:

Layer Greek Yogurt:
- Start by spooning a layer of Greek yogurt into the bottom of a glass or a bowl.

Add Granola Layer:
- Sprinkle a layer of granola over the Greek yogurt. You can use your favorite granola or one with nuts and dried fruits for added texture.

Add Fresh Berries:
- Add a layer of fresh berries on top of the granola. You can use a single type of berry or a mix for variety and color.

Repeat Layers:
- Repeat the layers by adding more Greek yogurt, granola, and berries until you reach the top of the glass or bowl.

Drizzle with Honey (Optional):
- If you like additional sweetness, drizzle honey or maple syrup over the top layer.

Top with Nuts or Seeds:
- Finish the parfait by sprinkling sliced almonds, chia seeds, or your favorite nuts and seeds on top for added crunch.

Serve:
- Serve the Greek Yogurt Parfait immediately as a healthy and satisfying breakfast or dessert.

Tips:

- Customize the parfait with your favorite fruits, nuts, or seeds.
- Experiment with flavored Greek yogurt for added variety.

Greek Yogurt Parfaits are not only delicious but also a great source of protein, probiotics, and fiber. They are versatile and can be enjoyed at any time of the day.

Whether you're looking for a quick and healthy breakfast or a light and refreshing dessert, a Greek Yogurt Parfait is a fantastic choice.

Stuffed Jalapeños

Ingredients:

- 12 fresh jalapeño peppers
- 8 ounces cream cheese, softened
- 1 cup shredded cheddar or Monterey Jack cheese
- 1/2 teaspoon garlic powder
- 1/2 teaspoon onion powder
- 1/2 teaspoon ground cumin
- Salt and black pepper to taste
- 12 slices of bacon, cut in half
- Toothpicks

Instructions:

Prepare the Jalapeños:
- Cut each jalapeño in half lengthwise and use a spoon to remove the seeds and membranes. Wear gloves to protect your hands from the spicy oils if desired.

Preheat the Oven:
- Preheat your oven to 375°F (190°C).

Prepare the Filling:
- In a mixing bowl, combine the softened cream cheese, shredded cheddar or Monterey Jack cheese, garlic powder, onion powder, ground cumin, salt, and black pepper. Mix until well combined.

Fill the Jalapeños:
- Spoon the cheese mixture into each jalapeño half, ensuring they are well-filled.

Wrap with Bacon:
- Wrap each stuffed jalapeño with a half-slice of bacon and secure it with a toothpick.

Arrange on a Baking Sheet:
- Place the stuffed jalapeños on a baking sheet lined with parchment paper.

Bake:
- Bake in the preheated oven for 20-25 minutes or until the bacon is crispy and the jalapeños are tender.

Broil (Optional):
- If the bacon needs more browning, you can broil the stuffed jalapeños for an additional 2-3 minutes, keeping a close eye to prevent burning.

Serve:
- Allow the stuffed jalapeños to cool slightly before serving. Remove the toothpicks and serve them as a spicy and savory appetizer.

Tips:

- Adjust the level of heat by leaving more or fewer seeds and membranes in the jalapeños.
- You can add additional ingredients to the filling, such as chopped herbs, cooked and crumbled sausage, or diced green onions.

Stuffed jalapeños are a crowd-pleasing appetizer, perfect for parties, game nights, or any occasion where you want to add a spicy kick to your menu.

Cucumber Slices with Cream Cheese

Ingredients:

- 1 large cucumber, washed and sliced into rounds
- 4 ounces (approximately 1/2 cup) cream cheese, softened
- Fresh dill, chopped (optional, for garnish)
- Salt and black pepper to taste

Instructions:

Prepare the Cucumber:
- Wash the cucumber thoroughly. You can peel it if you prefer or leave the skin on for added color and texture. Slice the cucumber into rounds, each about 1/4 to 1/2 inch thick.

Soften the Cream Cheese:
- Allow the cream cheese to soften at room temperature for easier spreading.

Spread Cream Cheese on Cucumber Slices:
- Using a small knife or a butter spreader, spread a layer of softened cream cheese onto each cucumber round.

Season with Salt and Pepper:
- Lightly sprinkle salt and black pepper over the cream cheese layer. Adjust the seasoning according to your taste.

Garnish with Fresh Dill (Optional):
- If you have fresh dill, sprinkle a bit over each cucumber and cream cheese slice for added flavor and garnish.

Serve:
- Arrange the cucumber slices with cream cheese on a serving platter.

Optional Variations:
- Feel free to experiment with additional toppings such as smoked salmon, chopped chives, or a dash of lemon zest.

Chill (Optional):
- For a cooler appetizer, refrigerate the cucumber slices with cream cheese for a short time before serving.

Tips:

- You can get creative with the presentation by arranging the cucumber slices in a circular pattern or stacking them for a more elegant look.
- This appetizer is best served fresh, so assemble it just before serving.

Cucumber slices with cream cheese make for a light and refreshing snack or appetizer, perfect for gatherings, brunches, or as a quick and healthy treat.

Buffalo Cauliflower Bites

Ingredients:

- 1 head of cauliflower, cut into florets
- 1 cup all-purpose flour
- 1 cup water
- 1 teaspoon garlic powder
- 1 teaspoon onion powder
- 1/2 teaspoon paprika
- Salt and black pepper to taste
- 1/2 cup buffalo sauce (store-bought or homemade)
- 2 tablespoons unsalted butter, melted
- Ranch or blue cheese dressing for dipping
- Celery sticks for serving (optional)

Instructions:

Preheat the Oven:
- Preheat your oven to 450°F (230°C). Line a baking sheet with parchment paper.

Prepare the Batter:
- In a mixing bowl, whisk together the flour, water, garlic powder, onion powder, paprika, salt, and black pepper until you have a smooth batter.

Coat Cauliflower Florets:
- Dip each cauliflower floret into the batter, ensuring it's well-coated, and then shake off any excess batter.

Bake the Cauliflower:
- Place the coated cauliflower florets on the prepared baking sheet. Bake in the preheated oven for 20-25 minutes or until they start to turn golden brown and crisp.

Prepare the Buffalo Sauce:
- While the cauliflower is baking, mix the buffalo sauce with melted butter in a separate bowl.

Toss in Buffalo Sauce:
- Once the cauliflower is done baking, transfer it to a large mixing bowl. Pour the buffalo sauce mixture over the cauliflower and toss until each piece is well-coated.

Bake Again:
- Return the cauliflower to the baking sheet and bake for an additional 10-15 minutes, allowing the sauce to caramelize and the cauliflower to become crispy.

Serve:

- Remove from the oven and let the Buffalo Cauliflower Bites cool slightly. Serve with ranch or blue cheese dressing for dipping and optional celery sticks.

Tips:

- Adjust the amount of buffalo sauce based on your spice preference.
- For an extra kick, add a pinch of cayenne pepper to the batter or buffalo sauce.

Buffalo Cauliflower Bites make a flavorful and crowd-pleasing appetizer or snack, especially for those who enjoy the bold flavors of buffalo wings. They're great for game nights, parties, or as a unique side dish.

Baked Sweet Potato Fries

Ingredients:

- 2 large sweet potatoes, peeled and cut into fries
- 2 tablespoons olive oil
- 1 teaspoon paprika
- 1/2 teaspoon garlic powder
- 1/2 teaspoon onion powder
- 1/2 teaspoon cumin
- Salt and black pepper to taste
- Optional: 1 tablespoon cornstarch (for extra crispiness)

Instructions:

Preheat the Oven:
- Preheat your oven to 425°F (220°C). Line a baking sheet with parchment paper or lightly grease it.

Prepare the Sweet Potatoes:
- Peel the sweet potatoes and cut them into evenly sized fries.

Coat with Olive Oil and Seasonings:
- In a large bowl, toss the sweet potato fries with olive oil, paprika, garlic powder, onion powder, cumin, salt, and black pepper. If you want extra crispiness, you can add cornstarch to the seasoning mix.

Arrange on Baking Sheet:
- Spread the seasoned sweet potato fries in a single layer on the prepared baking sheet, making sure they are not overcrowded. This helps them crisp up rather than steam.

Bake:
- Bake in the preheated oven for 20-25 minutes, flipping the fries halfway through the cooking time. Adjust the baking time as needed until the fries are golden brown and crispy.

Serve:
- Remove the sweet potato fries from the oven and let them cool slightly. Serve immediately and enjoy!

Tips:

- Feel free to customize the seasonings based on your taste preferences. You can add a pinch of cayenne pepper for heat or a sprinkle of cinnamon for a touch of sweetness.

- For even crispier fries, let the sweet potato fries soak in cold water for about 30 minutes before patting them dry and coating with the seasoning.

Baked sweet potato fries are a nutritious and flavorful side dish or snack. They are not only delicious but also rich in vitamins and fiber. Serve them alongside your favorite dipping sauce for a tasty and satisfying treat.

Bruschetta on Toasted Baguette

Ingredients:

- 4-5 ripe tomatoes, diced
- 1/4 cup fresh basil, chopped
- 2 cloves garlic, minced
- 2 tablespoons extra virgin olive oil
- Salt and black pepper to taste
- 1 baguette, sliced into rounds
- Optional: Balsamic glaze for drizzling

Instructions:

Preheat the Oven or Grill:
- Preheat your oven to 375°F (190°C) or use a grill.

Prepare the Tomato Mixture:
- In a bowl, combine diced tomatoes, chopped fresh basil, minced garlic, extra virgin olive oil, salt, and black pepper. Mix well to ensure the flavors are evenly distributed. Let it sit for a few minutes to allow the flavors to meld.

Toast the Baguette:
- Arrange the baguette slices on a baking sheet. Toast them in the preheated oven or on the grill until they are golden brown and crispy. This usually takes about 5-7 minutes in the oven or a couple of minutes on the grill. Keep an eye on them to prevent burning.

Top with Bruschetta Mixture:
- Once the baguette slices are toasted, spoon the tomato mixture generously over each slice. Make sure to include some of the tomato juices.

Optional Balsamic Glaze:
- Drizzle balsamic glaze over the bruschetta for an extra layer of flavor. This step is optional but adds a sweet and tangy element.

Serve:
- Arrange the Bruschetta on Toasted Baguette slices on a serving platter and serve immediately.

Tips:

- Rub the toasted baguette slices with a peeled garlic clove for an additional burst of garlic flavor.

- You can add a drizzle of high-quality balsamic glaze or reduction just before serving for a touch of sweetness.

Bruschetta on Toasted Baguette is a crowd-pleasing appetizer, perfect for parties, gatherings, or as a starter to a delicious Italian-inspired meal. The combination of fresh ingredients on crispy bread makes it a delightful and flavorful dish.

Cheese and Crackers Platter

Cheeses:

    Brie:
- Creamy and mild, Brie pairs well with both sweet and savory accompaniments.

    Cheddar:
- A classic choice with a sharp flavor, cheddar adds a robust element to the platter.

    Gouda:
- Smoked Gouda or aged Gouda brings a rich, nutty flavor to the mix.

    Blue Cheese:
- For a bold and tangy option, include blue cheese. Consider a milder variety if serving to a diverse group.

    Goat Cheese:
- Creamy and tangy, goat cheese complements fruits and honey.

Crackers and Bread:

    Water Crackers:
- These plain crackers provide a neutral base, allowing the cheese to shine.

    Multigrain Crackers:
- Add texture and a nutty flavor with multigrain or whole-grain crackers.

    Baguette Slices:
- Toasted baguette slices offer a crunchy alternative to crackers.

    Grilled or Seeded Bread:
- Include slices of grilled or seeded bread for additional variety.

Accompaniments:

    Fresh Fruits:
- Grapes, apple slices, or figs provide a sweet contrast to the savory cheeses.

    Dried Fruits:
- Apricots, dates, or figs add sweetness and chewiness.

    Nuts:
- Almonds, walnuts, or pecans bring a crunchy element to the platter.

    Honey or Fruit Preserves:
- A drizzle of honey or a dollop of fruit preserves complements the cheese.

    Olives:
- Green and black olives add a briny flavor.

    Mustard or Chutney:
- Spicy mustard or a flavorful chutney can enhance the overall experience.

Presentation:

- Arrange Artfully:
    - Arrange the cheeses, crackers, and accompaniments in an artful and visually appealing manner on a large platter or wooden board.
- Label Cheeses:
    - If serving a variety of cheeses, consider labeling them to help guests identify their favorites.
- Garnish with Fresh Herbs:
    - Add sprigs of fresh herbs like rosemary or thyme for a decorative touch.
- Serve at Room Temperature:
    - Allow cheeses to come to room temperature before serving for the best flavor.
- Provide Cheese Knives:
    - Place cheese knives or spreaders nearby for easy serving.

Tips:

- Choose a variety of textures and flavors for a well-rounded experience.
- Consider the preferences and dietary restrictions of your guests when selecting cheeses.

A well-crafted Cheese and Crackers Platter is not only a delicious appetizer but also a visually appealing centerpiece for any gathering or celebration. Customize it based on your preferences and the occasion.

Edamame with Sea Salt

Ingredients:

- 2 cups fresh or frozen edamame in pods
- Sea salt, to taste

Instructions:

Prepare Edamame:
- If using frozen edamame, follow the package instructions to thaw them. If using fresh edamame, rinse them under cold water.

Steam or Boil:
- Steam the edamame pods for about 5-7 minutes or boil them in lightly salted water for approximately 3-5 minutes until they are tender but still have a slight crunch.

Drain (if boiled):
- If boiled, drain the edamame and transfer them to a bowl.

Season with Sea Salt:
- While the edamame are still hot, sprinkle them generously with sea salt. Toss them to ensure the salt is evenly distributed.

Serve:
- Transfer the Edamame with Sea Salt to a serving bowl and serve immediately.

Tips:

- Customize the seasoning: Experiment with other seasonings such as garlic powder, chili flakes, or soy sauce for added flavor.
- Squeeze of lime: For a citrusy twist, consider squeezing fresh lime juice over the edamame before adding sea salt.

Edamame with Sea Salt is not only a tasty and satisfying snack but also a great source of plant-based protein, fiber, and various nutrients. Serve it as a healthy appetizer, snack, or a side dish for a wholesome treat.

Mini Quesadillas

Ingredients:

- 8 small flour tortillas
- 1 cup shredded cheese (cheddar, Monterey Jack, or a blend)
- 1 cup cooked and shredded chicken (optional)
- 1/2 cup diced tomatoes
- 1/4 cup diced red onions
- 1/4 cup chopped fresh cilantro
- 1 teaspoon taco seasoning (optional)
- Sour cream and salsa for serving

Instructions:

Prepare the Ingredients:
- Shred the cheese, dice the tomatoes, chop the onions, and shred the cooked chicken if using.

Assemble the Quesadillas:
- Lay out half of the tortillas and distribute the shredded cheese evenly over each one. If using chicken, add a small amount to each tortilla. Sprinkle tomatoes, red onions, and cilantro over the cheese.

Optional Taco Seasoning:
- If desired, sprinkle a pinch of taco seasoning over the ingredients for added flavor.

Top with Second Tortilla:
- Place the remaining tortillas on top to create mini quesadilla sandwiches.

Cook on Griddle or Pan:
- Heat a griddle or non-stick pan over medium heat. Cook each mini quesadilla for 2-3 minutes on each side, or until the tortillas are golden brown, and the cheese is melted.

Slice and Serve:
- Remove the mini quesadillas from the griddle and let them cool for a minute. Slice each one into quarters or smaller wedges.

Serve with Dipping Sauces:
- Serve the mini quesadillas with sour cream and salsa on the side for dipping.

Tips:

- Customize the filling: Feel free to add ingredients like black beans, corn, jalapeños, or any other favorite toppings.

- Make it vegetarian: Skip the chicken and focus on veggies and cheese for a delicious vegetarian option.

Mini quesadillas are a versatile and crowd-pleasing snack, perfect for casual gatherings, game nights, or as a tasty appetizer. They're quick to make and easy to customize according to your preferences.

Trail Mix with Nuts and Dried Fruits

Ingredients:

- 1 cup almonds, raw or roasted
- 1 cup walnuts or cashews
- 1/2 cup pumpkin seeds
- 1/2 cup sunflower seeds
- 1 cup mixed dried fruits (raisins, cranberries, apricots, cherries, etc.)
- 1/2 cup dark chocolate chips or chunks
- 1/2 cup coconut flakes (optional)
- 1/2 teaspoon salt (optional)

Instructions:

- Prepare the Nuts and Seeds:
  - If using raw nuts, you may choose to roast them in a dry skillet over medium heat for a few minutes until they become fragrant. Let them cool before mixing.
- Combine Ingredients:
  - In a large bowl, combine the almonds, walnuts or cashews, pumpkin seeds, sunflower seeds, mixed dried fruits, dark chocolate chips or chunks, and coconut flakes (if using).
- Add Salt (Optional):
  - If you like a hint of saltiness, you can sprinkle a little salt over the mix. Toss everything together until well combined.
- Store in an Airtight Container:
  - Transfer the trail mix to an airtight container or portion it into smaller snack-sized bags for convenient on-the-go options.
- Customize:
  - Feel free to customize your trail mix by adding your favorite nuts, seeds, or dried fruits. You can also experiment with different types of chocolate or include yogurt-covered nuts for a sweet twist.

Tips:

- For a sweet and salty combination, you can use salted nuts or add a touch of sea salt to the mix.
- Adjust the ratio of nuts to dried fruits based on your preference.
- Be mindful of portion sizes, as trail mix can be calorie-dense.

Trail mix with nuts and dried fruits is not only delicious but also provides a good balance of healthy fats, protein, and natural sugars. It's a convenient and satisfying snack to keep you fueled during your adventures or to combat those mid-afternoon cravings.

Smoked Salmon Crostini

Ingredients:

- Baguette, sliced into thin rounds
- 8 ounces cream cheese, softened
- 4 ounces smoked salmon, thinly sliced
- 2 tablespoons fresh dill, chopped
- 1 tablespoon capers, drained
- 1 tablespoon red onion, finely diced
- Lemon wedges, for serving
- Olive oil, for drizzling
- Salt and black pepper to taste

Instructions:

Preheat the Oven:
- Preheat your oven to 375°F (190°C).

Toast the Baguette:
- Place the baguette slices on a baking sheet and toast them in the preheated oven for 5-7 minutes or until they are golden and crisp.

Prepare the Cream Cheese:
- In a bowl, mix the softened cream cheese with chopped fresh dill. Season with salt and black pepper to taste.

Assemble the Crostini:
- Spread a generous layer of the dill-infused cream cheese onto each toasted baguette round.

Add Smoked Salmon:
- Place a slice of smoked salmon on top of the cream cheese layer, ensuring it covers the surface.

Garnish:
- Sprinkle finely diced red onion and capers over the smoked salmon.

Drizzle with Olive Oil:
- Drizzle a little olive oil over the assembled crostini for added richness.

Serve:
- Arrange the Smoked Salmon Crostini on a serving platter. Serve with lemon wedges on the side.

Tips:

- For extra flavor, you can mix a teaspoon of horseradish into the cream cheese.

- Experiment with different herbs, such as chives or parsley, for additional freshness.

Smoked Salmon Crostini is a sophisticated and crowd-pleasing appetizer, perfect for entertaining guests or enjoying a special occasion. The combination of creamy cheese, savory smoked salmon, and zesty accents creates a delightful flavor profile that's sure to impress.

Baked Zucchini Chips

Ingredients:

- 2 medium zucchini, thinly sliced
- 2 tablespoons olive oil
- 1/2 cup breadcrumbs (preferably seasoned)
- 1/4 cup grated Parmesan cheese
- 1/2 teaspoon garlic powder
- 1/2 teaspoon onion powder
- 1/2 teaspoon dried oregano
- Salt and black pepper to taste
- Cooking spray

Instructions:

Preheat the Oven:
- Preheat your oven to 425°F (220°C). Line a baking sheet with parchment paper and lightly coat it with cooking spray.

Prepare Zucchini:
- Wash and dry the zucchini. Slice it into thin rounds, about 1/8 inch thick. Pat the slices dry with a paper towel to remove excess moisture.

Prepare Coating Mixture:
- In a bowl, combine breadcrumbs, grated Parmesan cheese, garlic powder, onion powder, dried oregano, salt, and black pepper. Mix well.

Coat Zucchini Slices:
- Dip each zucchini slice into the olive oil, ensuring both sides are lightly coated. Then, dip the slices into the breadcrumb mixture, pressing gently to adhere the coating.

Place on Baking Sheet:
- Arrange the coated zucchini slices on the prepared baking sheet in a single layer, making sure they are not touching.

Bake:
- Bake in the preheated oven for 15-20 minutes or until the zucchini chips are golden brown and crispy. Flip the chips halfway through the baking time to ensure even cooking.

Serve:
- Once the zucchini chips are done, remove them from the oven and let them cool for a few minutes. Serve immediately as a crunchy and satisfying snack.

Tips:

- Experiment with different seasonings like paprika, cayenne pepper, or Italian seasoning for added flavor.
- Keep an eye on the chips towards the end of the baking time to prevent them from overcooking and becoming too brown.

Baked zucchini chips are a nutritious and tasty way to enjoy a crunchy snack. They are great for satisfying cravings while providing the benefits of zucchini's vitamins and minerals. Serve them as an appetizer, side dish, or a guilt-free snack.

Chicken Satay Skewers

Ingredients:

For the Chicken Marinade:

- 1.5 lbs (700g) boneless, skinless chicken thighs, cut into strips
- 2 tablespoons soy sauce
- 2 tablespoons fish sauce
- 2 tablespoons brown sugar
- 2 tablespoons vegetable oil
- 1 tablespoon curry powder
- 1 teaspoon ground turmeric
- 2 cloves garlic, minced
- 1 tablespoon lemongrass, minced (optional)
- Wooden skewers, soaked in water for 30 minutes

For the Peanut Sauce:

- 1/2 cup peanut butter
- 2 tablespoons soy sauce
- 1 tablespoon brown sugar
- 1 tablespoon lime juice
- 1 teaspoon sesame oil
- 1 teaspoon Sriracha sauce (adjust to taste)
- 1/2 cup coconut milk
- Chopped peanuts and cilantro for garnish (optional)

Instructions:

Prepare the Marinade:
- In a bowl, whisk together soy sauce, fish sauce, brown sugar, vegetable oil, curry powder, turmeric, minced garlic, and lemongrass (if using).

Marinate the Chicken:
- Place the chicken strips in the marinade, ensuring they are well-coated. Cover and refrigerate for at least 30 minutes to let the flavors meld.

Preheat the Grill or Oven:
- Preheat your grill or oven to medium-high heat.

Skewer the Chicken:
- Thread the marinated chicken strips onto the soaked wooden skewers.

Grill or Bake:

- Grill the chicken skewers for 5-7 minutes on each side or until they are cooked through and have a nice char. Alternatively, you can bake them in the oven at 400°F (200°C) for about 15-20 minutes, flipping halfway through.

Prepare Peanut Sauce:
- While the chicken is cooking, make the peanut sauce. In a small saucepan, combine peanut butter, soy sauce, brown sugar, lime juice, sesame oil, Sriracha, and coconut milk. Heat over medium heat, stirring continuously until well combined and heated through.

Serve:
- Serve the grilled chicken satay skewers with the peanut sauce on the side. Garnish with chopped peanuts and cilantro if desired.

Tips:

- Adjust the level of spiciness by modifying the amount of Sriracha in the peanut sauce.
- If using wooden skewers, soak them in water for at least 30 minutes before threading the chicken to prevent them from burning during grilling.

Chicken satay skewers are perfect for serving as an appetizer, snack, or part of a main meal. The combination of tender, flavorful chicken with the rich and nutty peanut sauce makes for a delightful and satisfying dish.

Sliced Apple with Peanut Butter

Ingredients:

- 1-2 medium-sized apples (variety of your choice)
- Peanut butter (smooth or crunchy)

Instructions:

> Select and Wash Apples:
> - Choose your favorite variety of apples, such as Granny Smith, Honeycrisp, or Fuji. Wash the apples thoroughly under running water.
>
> Slice the Apples:
> - Core the apples and slice them into thin, manageable rounds or wedges. You can leave the skin on for added fiber and nutrients.
>
> Serve with Peanut Butter:
> - Scoop a generous dollop of peanut butter onto a small plate or bowl.
>
> Dip or Spread:
> - Dip the apple slices directly into the peanut butter or use a knife to spread the peanut butter onto each apple slice.
>
> Enjoy:
> - Bite into the delicious combination of crisp apple and creamy peanut butter. The contrast of textures and flavors makes for a satisfying and nutritious snack.

Tips:

- Experiment with different types of nut or seed butters if you have allergies or dietary preferences.
- Enhance the snack by sprinkling a pinch of cinnamon or a drizzle of honey over the apple slices.

Sliced apples with peanut butter is a classic and well-balanced snack that provides a mix of natural sugars, healthy fats, and fiber. It's not only delicious but also a great option for a quick energy boost or a satisfying treat during any time of the day.

Mini Meatballs with Dipping Sauce

Ingredients:

For the Meatballs:

- 1 pound ground beef or a mix of beef and pork
- 1/2 cup breadcrumbs
- 1/4 cup grated Parmesan cheese
- 1/4 cup chopped fresh parsley
- 2 cloves garlic, minced
- 1 egg
- Salt and black pepper to taste
- Cooking spray

For the Dipping Sauce:

- 1/2 cup ketchup
- 2 tablespoons soy sauce
- 1 tablespoon honey
- 1 teaspoon Dijon mustard
- 1/2 teaspoon garlic powder
- 1/2 teaspoon onion powder

Instructions:

Preheat the Oven:
- Preheat your oven to 375°F (190°C).

Prepare the Meatball Mixture:
- In a bowl, combine ground beef, breadcrumbs, grated Parmesan, chopped parsley, minced garlic, egg, salt, and black pepper. Mix until well combined.

Shape into Mini Meatballs:
- Shape the mixture into small meatballs, about 1 inch in diameter.

Bake the Meatballs:
- Place the mini meatballs on a baking sheet lined with parchment paper and lightly coated with cooking spray. Bake in the preheated oven for 15-20 minutes or until the meatballs are cooked through and golden brown.

Prepare the Dipping Sauce:
- While the meatballs are baking, make the dipping sauce. In a small saucepan, combine ketchup, soy sauce, honey, Dijon mustard, garlic powder, and onion

powder. Heat over medium heat, stirring continuously until well combined and heated through.

Serve:
- Once the meatballs are done, transfer them to a serving platter and serve with toothpicks for easy dipping. Drizzle the dipping sauce over the meatballs or serve it on the side.

Tips:

- Customize the meatball mixture by adding herbs like oregano or thyme for extra flavor.
- Adjust the sweetness and saltiness of the dipping sauce to your taste by modifying the honey and soy sauce quantities.

These Mini Meatballs with Dipping Sauce are perfect for parties, game nights, or any social gathering. The combination of savory meatballs and a sweet-savory dipping sauce is sure to be a hit with your guests.

Rice Cake with Avocado and Radish

Ingredients:

- Rice cakes
- 1 ripe avocado
- Radishes, thinly sliced
- Lemon or lime juice
- Salt and black pepper to taste
- Optional: Red pepper flakes, sesame seeds, or fresh herbs for garnish

Instructions:

Prepare the Avocado:
- Cut the ripe avocado in half, remove the pit, and scoop the flesh into a bowl.

Mash the Avocado:
- Mash the avocado with a fork until it reaches your desired level of creaminess. Add a squeeze of lemon or lime juice to prevent browning.

Season the Avocado:
- Season the mashed avocado with salt and black pepper to taste. Adjust the seasoning according to your preferences.

Assemble the Rice Cakes:
- Spread a generous layer of mashed avocado onto each rice cake.

Add Sliced Radishes:
- Arrange thinly sliced radishes on top of the mashed avocado layer.

Garnish (Optional):
- Sprinkle red pepper flakes, sesame seeds, or fresh herbs for additional flavor and visual appeal.

Serve:
- Place the rice cakes with avocado and radish on a plate and serve immediately.

Tips:

- Enhance the flavor by adding a drizzle of olive oil or a sprinkle of your favorite seasoning blend.
- Experiment with different types of radishes, such as watermelon radishes or daikon, for varied colors and textures.

Rice cakes with avocado and radish are a delightful combination of creamy, crunchy, and refreshing elements. This snack is not only quick to prepare but also provides a good balance of healthy fats, fiber, and vitamins. It's perfect for a light breakfast, snack, or as part of a wholesome lunch.

Chocolate-Dipped Strawberries

Ingredients:

- Fresh strawberries, washed and dried
- Dark, milk, or white chocolate (or a combination)
- Optional: Chopped nuts, shredded coconut, or sprinkles for decoration

Instructions:

Prepare the Strawberries:
- Make sure the strawberries are thoroughly washed and dried. Pat them dry with paper towels to remove excess moisture.

Melt the Chocolate:
- Chop the chocolate into small, uniform pieces. Place it in a heatproof bowl. You can melt the chocolate using one of the following methods:
    - Double Boiler: Place the bowl over a pot of simmering water, ensuring the water doesn't touch the bottom of the bowl. Stir the chocolate until completely melted.
    - Microwave: Microwave the chocolate in 20-30 second intervals, stirring between each interval until melted.

Dip the Strawberries:
- Hold each strawberry by the stem and dip it into the melted chocolate, covering about two-thirds of the strawberry. Allow any excess chocolate to drip off.

Decorate (Optional):
- While the chocolate is still wet, you can sprinkle chopped nuts, shredded coconut, or colorful sprinkles over the dipped part of the strawberry for added texture and flavor.

Place on Parchment Paper:
- Lay the chocolate-dipped strawberries on a parchment paper-lined tray or plate. Ensure they are not touching each other.

Set the Chocolate:
- Allow the chocolate on the strawberries to set. You can speed up the process by placing the tray in the refrigerator for about 15-20 minutes.

Serve:
- Once the chocolate has hardened, carefully transfer the chocolate-dipped strawberries to a serving platter. Serve and enjoy!

Tips:

- Use high-quality chocolate for the best flavor and texture.
- Get creative with decorations – try drizzling melted white chocolate over dark chocolate-dipped strawberries for a decorative touch.
- Serve the chocolate-dipped strawberries the same day for the freshest taste and texture.

Chocolate-dipped strawberries are a classic and delightful treat that combines the sweetness of ripe strawberries with the richness of chocolate. They make for a lovely dessert, a sweet gift, or a beautiful addition to special occasions.

Stuffed Mushrooms

Ingredients:

- 12-15 large white or cremini mushrooms, cleaned and stems removed
- 1/2 cup breadcrumbs
- 1/2 cup grated Parmesan cheese
- 1/4 cup chopped fresh parsley
- 2 cloves garlic, minced
- 1/4 cup melted butter or olive oil
- Salt and black pepper to taste
- Optional: Chopped bacon, sausage, or herbs for additional flavor

Instructions:

Prepare the Mushrooms:
- Preheat the oven to 375°F (190°C). Clean the mushrooms with a damp cloth or paper towel to remove any dirt. Gently twist or use a spoon to remove the stems, creating a cavity for the stuffing.

Prepare the Filling:
- In a bowl, combine breadcrumbs, grated Parmesan cheese, chopped parsley, minced garlic, and any optional ingredients such as chopped bacon or cooked sausage. Mix well.

Season the Filling:
- Season the filling mixture with salt and black pepper to taste. Adjust the seasoning according to your preferences.

Stuff the Mushrooms:
- Using a spoon or your fingers, stuff each mushroom cap with the prepared filling, pressing it down gently.

Arrange on a Baking Sheet:
- Place the stuffed mushrooms on a baking sheet lined with parchment paper, ensuring they are evenly spaced.

Drizzle with Butter or Olive Oil:
- Drizzle melted butter or olive oil over the stuffed mushrooms. This adds moisture and enhances the flavor.

Bake:
- Bake in the preheated oven for approximately 15-20 minutes or until the mushrooms are tender and the filling is golden brown.

Serve Warm:

- Once baked, remove the stuffed mushrooms from the oven. Allow them to cool slightly before serving.

Tips:

- Experiment with different cheeses, such as mozzarella or feta, for varied flavors.
- Customize the filling by adding finely chopped herbs like thyme, rosemary, or chives.

Stuffed mushrooms are a versatile appetizer that you can tailor to your taste preferences. They are perfect for parties, gatherings, or as a tasty addition to your appetizer spread.

Pita Bread with Tzatziki

Ingredients:

For Tzatziki:

- 1 cup Greek yogurt
- 1/2 cucumber, finely grated and drained
- 2 cloves garlic, minced
- 1 tablespoon fresh dill, chopped
- 1 tablespoon fresh mint, chopped (optional)
- 1 tablespoon extra-virgin olive oil
- 1 teaspoon lemon juice
- Salt and black pepper to taste

For Serving:

- Pita bread (white or whole wheat)
- Cherry tomatoes, sliced cucumbers, red onion rings (optional)

Instructions:

Prepare Tzatziki:
- In a bowl, combine Greek yogurt, finely grated and drained cucumber, minced garlic, chopped dill, chopped mint (if using), olive oil, lemon juice, salt, and black pepper. Mix well to combine.

Chill Tzatziki:
- Cover the bowl with plastic wrap and refrigerate the tzatziki for at least 30 minutes to allow the flavors to meld.

Warm Pita Bread:
- If using store-bought pita bread, warm it in a toaster, oven, or on a skillet for a minute or two until it becomes soft and pliable.

Assemble:
- Spread a generous amount of tzatziki onto the warmed pita bread.

Optional Toppings:
- Add additional toppings like sliced cherry tomatoes, cucumber slices, and red onion rings for extra freshness and crunch.

Serve:
- Fold the pita in half or roll it up, creating a delicious pita pocket. Serve immediately.

Tips:

- Customize the tzatziki by adjusting the garlic, lemon, or herb quantities to suit your taste.
- For a heartier meal, add grilled chicken, lamb, or falafel to the pita bread.

Pita bread with tzatziki is a light and satisfying dish, perfect for a quick lunch, snack, or as part of a Mediterranean-inspired spread. The creamy and herby tzatziki complements the softness of the pita bread, creating a delightful combination of textures and flavors.

Greek Spanakopita Triangles

Ingredients:

For the Filling:

- 1 pound (450g) fresh spinach, washed and chopped
- 1 cup feta cheese, crumbled
- 1 cup ricotta cheese
- 1/2 cup grated Parmesan cheese
- 1 small onion, finely chopped
- 2 cloves garlic, minced
- 2 tablespoons olive oil
- Salt and black pepper to taste
- 1/2 teaspoon nutmeg (optional)

For the Pastry:

- 1 package (about 40 sheets) phyllo dough, thawed if frozen
- 1/2 cup unsalted butter, melted

Instructions:

Prepare the Filling:
- In a large skillet, heat olive oil over medium heat. Add chopped onions and minced garlic, sautéing until softened.
- Add chopped spinach to the skillet and cook until wilted. Drain any excess liquid.
- In a large bowl, combine the cooked spinach mixture with crumbled feta, ricotta, Parmesan, salt, black pepper, and nutmeg. Mix well.

Preheat the Oven:
- Preheat your oven to 375°F (190°C).

Assemble the Triangles:
- Lay out one sheet of phyllo dough and brush it lightly with melted butter. Place another sheet on top and brush with butter again. Repeat this process until you have about 4-5 layers.
- Cut the layered phyllo into strips or squares, depending on your preference.
- Place a spoonful of the spinach and feta mixture at one end of each strip or square.

- Fold the pastry over the filling to form a triangle, continuing to fold until you reach the end of the strip or square. Repeat this process with the remaining phyllo and filling.

Bake:
- Place the assembled triangles on a baking sheet and brush the tops with melted butter.
- Bake in the preheated oven for 20-25 minutes or until the triangles are golden brown and crispy.

Serve:
- Allow the Spanakopita triangles to cool for a few minutes before serving. They can be enjoyed warm or at room temperature.

Tips:

- Keep the phyllo dough covered with a damp kitchen towel while working to prevent it from drying out.
- Experiment with additional herbs like dill or mint for added flavor in the filling.

These Greek Spanakopita triangles are perfect as appetizers, party snacks, or a delightful addition to a Mediterranean-themed meal. The combination of flaky phyllo pastry and the savory spinach and feta filling creates a delicious and impressive treat.

Roasted Chickpeas

Ingredients:

- 2 cans (15 ounces each) chickpeas (garbanzo beans), drained and rinsed
- 2 tablespoons olive oil
- 1 teaspoon ground cumin
- 1 teaspoon smoked paprika
- 1/2 teaspoon garlic powder
- 1/2 teaspoon onion powder
- 1/4 teaspoon cayenne pepper (adjust to taste)
- Salt and black pepper to taste

Instructions:

Preheat the Oven:
- Preheat your oven to 400°F (200°C).

Dry Chickpeas:
- After draining and rinsing the chickpeas, pat them dry with a clean kitchen towel or paper towels. Removing excess moisture helps in achieving a crispy texture.

Season Chickpeas:
- In a bowl, toss the chickpeas with olive oil, ground cumin, smoked paprika, garlic powder, onion powder, cayenne pepper, salt, and black pepper. Ensure the chickpeas are evenly coated with the seasonings.

Spread on Baking Sheet:
- Spread the seasoned chickpeas in a single layer on a baking sheet lined with parchment paper or a silicone baking mat. This allows for even roasting.

Roast in the Oven:
- Roast the chickpeas in the preheated oven for 25-35 minutes or until they are golden brown and crispy. Shake the baking sheet or stir the chickpeas halfway through the cooking time for even results.

Cool and Serve:
- Allow the roasted chickpeas to cool on the baking sheet for a few minutes. They will continue to crisp up as they cool. Once cooled, transfer them to a bowl and serve.

Tips:

- Experiment with different seasonings like curry powder, chili powder, or your favorite spice blend.
- Store leftover roasted chickpeas in an airtight container. They are best enjoyed within a day or two to maintain their crunchiness.

Roasted chickpeas are a versatile and nutritious snack that provides a satisfying crunch. They are also a great alternative to traditional snacks and can be seasoned to suit various flavor preferences. Enjoy them on their own or use them as a topping for salads and soups!

Shrimp Cocktail

Ingredients:

For the Shrimp:

- 1 pound large shrimp, peeled and deveined (with tails on or off)
- 1 tablespoon olive oil
- Salt and black pepper to taste
- Lemon wedges for garnish

For the Cocktail Sauce:

- 1/2 cup ketchup
- 2 tablespoons prepared horseradish (adjust to taste)
- 1 tablespoon Worcestershire sauce
- 1 tablespoon fresh lemon juice
- 1 teaspoon hot sauce (optional)
- Salt and black pepper to taste

Instructions:

Cook the Shrimp:
- Bring a large pot of salted water to a boil. Add the shrimp and cook for 2-3 minutes or until they turn pink and opaque. Be careful not to overcook, as shrimp can become rubbery.

Drain and Chill:
- Drain the cooked shrimp and transfer them immediately to an ice bath to stop the cooking process. Once cooled, drain again and refrigerate until ready to serve.

Prepare the Cocktail Sauce:
- In a bowl, mix together ketchup, horseradish, Worcestershire sauce, fresh lemon juice, hot sauce (if using), salt, and black pepper. Adjust the horseradish and hot sauce quantities to your taste preferences.

Chill the Sauce:
- Cover the cocktail sauce and refrigerate for at least 30 minutes to allow the flavors to meld.

Serve:
- Arrange the chilled shrimp on a serving platter with lemon wedges on the side. Place a small bowl of the cocktail sauce in the center for dipping.

Tips:

- For added presentation, you can line the serving platter with shredded lettuce or fresh herbs.
- Customize the cocktail sauce by adding a dash of Tabasco, grated horseradish, or a splash of vodka for extra flavor.

Shrimp cocktail is a timeless and elegant appetizer that's perfect for entertaining or as a refreshing starter. The combination of tender, chilled shrimp with zesty cocktail sauce is a delightful treat for any occasion.

Brussel Sprout Chips

Ingredients:

- 1 pound Brussels sprouts, trimmed and outer leaves removed
- 2 tablespoons olive oil
- Salt and black pepper to taste
- Optional: Grated Parmesan cheese, garlic powder, or smoked paprika for extra flavor

Instructions:

    Preheat the Oven:
- Preheat your oven to 375°F (190°C).

    Prepare Brussels Sprouts:
- Trim the ends of the Brussels sprouts and remove any yellow or damaged outer leaves. Cut the sprouts in half lengthwise.

    Toss with Olive Oil:
- In a large bowl, toss the Brussels sprout halves with olive oil, ensuring they are well-coated.

    Season:
- Season the Brussels sprouts with salt and black pepper. You can also add optional seasonings like grated Parmesan cheese, garlic powder, or smoked paprika for extra flavor.

    Arrange on Baking Sheet:
- Spread the seasoned Brussels sprouts in a single layer on a baking sheet lined with parchment paper.

    Bake:
- Bake in the preheated oven for 15-20 minutes or until the Brussels sprout leaves are crispy and golden brown. Be sure to check them frequently to prevent burning.

    Cool and Serve:
- Allow the Brussels sprout chips to cool for a few minutes on the baking sheet before serving. They will continue to crisp up as they cool.

Tips:

- Make sure the Brussels sprouts are thoroughly dry before tossing them with olive oil to ensure crispiness.
- Experiment with different seasonings to customize the flavor of your Brussels sprout chips.

Brussels sprout chips are a delicious and healthier snack option. They're packed with nutrients and offer a satisfying crunch. Enjoy them on their own or as a tasty side dish!

Mini Tacos with Guacamole

Ingredients:

For Mini Tacos:

- Mini taco shells or tortilla scoops
- 1 pound ground beef or chicken
- 1 packet taco seasoning
- 1 cup shredded lettuce
- 1 cup diced tomatoes
- 1 cup shredded cheese (cheddar or Mexican blend)
- Sour cream for garnish
- Fresh cilantro for garnish (optional)

For Guacamole:

- 2 ripe avocados
- 1 small onion, finely diced
- 1 tomato, diced
- 1 lime, juiced
- Salt and black pepper to taste
- Optional: Jalapeño, finely chopped, for heat
- Optional: Garlic powder, cumin, or cayenne for additional flavor

Instructions:

For Guacamole:

Prepare Guacamole:
- In a bowl, mash the ripe avocados with a fork.
- Add finely diced onion, diced tomato, lime juice, salt, black pepper, and any optional ingredients like jalapeño, garlic powder, cumin, or cayenne. Mix well to combine.

Adjust Seasoning:
- Taste the guacamole and adjust the seasoning or lime juice according to your preferences. Cover with plastic wrap, pressing it directly onto the surface of the guacamole to prevent browning. Refrigerate until ready to use.

For Mini Tacos:

Cook Ground Meat:
- In a skillet over medium heat, cook the ground beef or chicken until fully browned. Drain any excess fat.

Season with Taco Seasoning:
- Add the taco seasoning to the cooked meat according to the package instructions. Mix well and let it simmer for a few minutes.

Assemble Mini Tacos:
- Fill each mini taco shell or tortilla scoop with a spoonful of the seasoned meat.

Add Toppings:
- Top the mini tacos with shredded lettuce, diced tomatoes, shredded cheese, and a dollop of guacamole.

Garnish and Serve:
- Garnish the mini tacos with a drizzle of sour cream and fresh cilantro, if desired. Serve immediately.

Tips:

- Customize the taco filling by adding beans, corn, or sautéed peppers and onions.
- For a vegetarian version, replace the meat with seasoned black beans or grilled vegetables.

These Mini Tacos with Guacamole are not only visually appealing but also bursting with flavors. They are perfect for entertaining guests or as a fun and tasty snack for any occasion.

Mango Salsa with Tortilla Chips

Ingredients:

- 2 ripe mangoes, peeled, pitted, and diced
- 1/2 red onion, finely chopped
- 1 jalapeño, seeds removed and finely chopped
- 1 red bell pepper, diced
- 1/4 cup fresh cilantro, chopped
- Juice of 2 limes
- Salt and black pepper to taste

Instructions:

> Prepare the Mangoes:
> - Peel, pit, and dice the ripe mangoes. Ensure they are ripe but still firm.
>
> Chop Vegetables:
> - Finely chop the red onion, jalapeño (seeds removed for milder heat), red bell pepper, and fresh cilantro.
>
> Combine Ingredients:
> - In a bowl, combine the diced mangoes, chopped red onion, jalapeño, red bell pepper, and cilantro.
>
> Add Lime Juice:
> - Squeeze the juice of two limes over the mixture. Adjust the amount of lime juice to your taste preferences.
>
> Season:
> - Season the mango salsa with salt and black pepper. Toss gently to combine all the ingredients.
>
> Chill:
> - Cover the bowl with plastic wrap and refrigerate the mango salsa for at least 30 minutes to allow the flavors to meld.

Tortilla Chips:

- Store-bought tortilla chips or homemade tortilla chips (cut corn tortillas into triangles, brush with olive oil, sprinkle with salt, and bake until crispy).

Assembly:

> Serve:

- Just before serving, give the mango salsa a final toss and adjust the seasoning if needed.

Pair with Tortilla Chips:
- Serve the mango salsa in a bowl alongside your favorite tortilla chips.

Garnish (Optional):
- Garnish the mango salsa with additional cilantro or lime wedges if desired.

Tips:

- For variation, consider adding diced avocado or a small amount of finely chopped red cabbage for extra color and texture.
- Make the mango salsa ahead of time and refrigerate, but add the cilantro just before serving to maintain its freshness.

Mango salsa with tortilla chips is a crowd-pleasing and vibrant appetizer that combines the sweetness of mangoes with the heat of jalapeño and the freshness of cilantro. It's perfect for parties, barbecues, or as a light and refreshing snack on a warm day.

Crab Rangoon

Ingredients:

- 8 oz (about 1 cup) crab meat, canned or fresh, drained
- 8 oz cream cheese, softened
- 2 green onions, finely chopped
- 1 clove garlic, minced
- 1 teaspoon soy sauce
- 1/2 teaspoon Worcestershire sauce
- 1/4 teaspoon sesame oil
- 1/4 teaspoon black pepper
- Wonton wrappers
- Vegetable oil for frying

Instructions:

Prepare the Filling:
- In a bowl, combine the drained crab meat, softened cream cheese, chopped green onions, minced garlic, soy sauce, Worcestershire sauce, sesame oil, and black pepper. Mix well until the ingredients are evenly incorporated.

Assemble the Crab Rangoon:
- Lay out a wonton wrapper on a clean surface. Place a teaspoon of the crab and cream cheese mixture in the center of the wrapper.

Moisten Edges:
- Moisten the edges of the wonton wrapper with water using your fingertip. This helps seal the edges.

Fold and Seal:
- Fold the wonton wrapper in half diagonally, creating a triangle. Press the edges to seal, ensuring there are no air pockets.

Form the Crab Rangoon:
- Optionally, you can fold the two bottom corners of the triangle together, forming a hat-like shape. Press to seal.

Repeat:
- Repeat the process with the remaining wonton wrappers and filling.

Heat Oil:
- In a deep fryer or a large, deep skillet, heat vegetable oil to 350°F (180°C).

Fry the Crab Rangoon:

- Carefully place a few Crab Rangoon at a time into the hot oil and fry until golden brown, about 2-3 minutes. Ensure even cooking by turning them halfway through the frying process.

Drain and Serve:

- Use a slotted spoon to remove the fried Crab Rangoon from the oil and place them on a paper towel-lined plate to drain excess oil.

Serve Warm:

- Serve the Crab Rangoon warm, and optionally, with sweet and sour sauce or soy sauce for dipping.

Tips:

- Ensure the cream cheese is softened for easy mixing and a smoother filling.
- Experiment with different folding styles for a decorative touch.

Homemade Crab Rangoon is a delicious and crispy appetizer that's sure to be a hit at parties or as a savory snack. Enjoy the creamy and flavorful filling encased in a crispy golden shell!

Cherry Tomato and Mozzarella Bites

Ingredients:

- Cherry tomatoes
- Fresh mozzarella balls (bocconcini)
- Fresh basil leaves
- Balsamic glaze or balsamic reduction
- Toothpicks or small skewers
- Olive oil (optional)
- Salt and black pepper to taste

Instructions:

Prepare Ingredients:
- Wash the cherry tomatoes and basil leaves. Drain the mozzarella balls if stored in liquid.

Assemble the Bites:
- On each toothpick or skewer, thread a cherry tomato, a folded basil leaf, and a mozzarella ball.

Arrange on a Platter:
- Arrange the assembled bites on a serving platter.

Drizzle with Balsamic Glaze:
- Drizzle balsamic glaze or balsamic reduction over the cherry tomato and mozzarella bites. Alternatively, you can use a toothpick to carefully dip each bite into the balsamic glaze.

Optional: Season with Olive Oil:
- If desired, you can also drizzle a small amount of olive oil over the bites. This adds an extra layer of richness.

Season with Salt and Pepper:
- Season the bites with a pinch of salt and black pepper to taste.

Serve:
- Serve the cherry tomato and mozzarella bites immediately. They are best enjoyed fresh.

Tips:

- Choose ripe and sweet cherry tomatoes for the best flavor.
- Use fresh basil leaves to enhance the aroma and taste of the bites.
- If you prefer, you can marinate the mozzarella balls in olive oil, garlic, and herbs for added flavor.

Cherry tomato and mozzarella bites are a classic and elegant appetizer that's perfect for gatherings, parties, or as a light and refreshing snack. The combination of sweet tomatoes, creamy mozzarella, and aromatic basil creates a burst of flavors in every bite.

Artisanal Cheese Plate

Cheeses:

- Soft Cheese:
  - Choose a creamy and soft cheese like Brie, Camembert, or goat cheese. This provides a rich and mild option for your plate.
- Semi-Soft Cheese:
  - Include a semi-soft cheese such as Gouda, Havarti, or Fontina. These cheeses have a slightly firmer texture and often come in various flavors.
- Hard Cheese:
  - Add a hard cheese for a more robust and aged flavor. Examples include Cheddar, Gruyere, or Manchego.
- Blue Cheese:
  - For a bold and distinctive taste, include a blue cheese like Roquefort, Stilton, or Gorgonzola. This adds a tangy and savory element to the plate.

Accompaniments:

- Fresh and Dried Fruits:
  - Slice fresh fruits like apples, pears, or grapes. Additionally, include dried fruits such as apricots or figs for a sweet contrast.
- Nuts:
  - Choose a variety of nuts like almonds, walnuts, or pecans. Toasted nuts can add an extra layer of flavor.
- Crackers and Bread:
  - Offer a selection of crackers and bread, such as baguette slices, crispbreads, or artisanal crackers. These serve as a neutral base for the cheeses.
- Honey or Fruit Preserves:
  - Provide honey or fruit preserves to add sweetness. The natural sweetness of honey complements the savory notes of the cheeses.
- Olives and Pickles:
  - Include a variety of olives or pickles for a salty and briny component. This can balance the richness of the cheeses.
- Cured Meats (Optional):
  - If you'd like to include meats, add cured options like prosciutto, salami, or chorizo. These add a savory element to the plate.

Presentation:

- Arrange the Cheeses:

- Place the cheeses on the board, leaving space between each variety. Consider slicing or cubing some of the cheeses for easier serving.

Create Sections:
- Arrange accompaniments in designated sections around the cheeses. This makes it visually appealing and easy for guests to pair flavors.

Garnish (Optional):
- Garnish the board with fresh herbs, edible flowers, or decorative elements to enhance the presentation.

Serve at Room Temperature:
- Take the cheeses out of the refrigerator at least an hour before serving to allow them to come to room temperature. This enhances their flavors and textures.

Label the Cheeses (Optional):
- Consider providing small labels with the names of the cheeses to guide your guests and encourage exploration.

Tips:

- Experiment with different textures, flavors, and types of cheeses to create a diverse tasting experience.
- Consider wine pairings or accompaniments that complement specific cheeses.

An artisanal cheese plate offers a delightful and interactive experience for your guests, allowing them to savor a variety of flavors and textures. Customize the plate based on your preferences and the season for a memorable culinary treat.

Teriyaki Chicken Skewers

Ingredients:

For the Teriyaki Marinade:

- 1/2 cup soy sauce
- 1/4 cup mirin (sweet rice wine)
- 2 tablespoons sake or white wine
- 2 tablespoons brown sugar
- 2 cloves garlic, minced
- 1 teaspoon ginger, grated
- 1 tablespoon honey (optional, for extra sweetness)
- 1.5 to 2 pounds boneless, skinless chicken thighs, cut into bite-sized pieces

For Skewers:

- Bamboo skewers, soaked in water for at least 30 minutes
- Sesame seeds for garnish (optional)
- Sliced green onions for garnish (optional)

Instructions:

Prepare the Teriyaki Marinade:
- In a bowl, whisk together soy sauce, mirin, sake (or white wine), brown sugar, minced garlic, grated ginger, and honey (if using). This creates the teriyaki marinade.

Marinate the Chicken:
- Place the chicken pieces in a shallow dish or a zip-top bag. Pour half of the teriyaki marinade over the chicken, ensuring each piece is coated. Reserve the other half for basting and serving later.

Marinate Time:
- Marinate the chicken in the refrigerator for at least 30 minutes to allow the flavors to infuse. For a deeper flavor, you can marinate for several hours or overnight.

Skewer the Chicken:
- Preheat your grill or oven broiler. Thread the marinated chicken pieces onto the soaked bamboo skewers.

Grill or Broil:

- Grill the chicken skewers over medium-high heat for 6-8 minutes, turning occasionally, or until the chicken is cooked through and has a nice char. Alternatively, you can broil them in the oven, turning halfway through.

Baste with Marinade:
- During the last few minutes of cooking, baste the chicken skewers with the reserved teriyaki marinade, ensuring a glossy finish.

Garnish and Serve:
- Once cooked, transfer the skewers to a serving platter. Garnish with sesame seeds and sliced green onions if desired.

Serve with Rice or Vegetables:
- Serve the teriyaki chicken skewers over steamed rice or with your favorite vegetables.

Tips:

- Customize the marinade by adding a splash of pineapple juice for a tropical twist.
- If using wooden skewers, soak them in water for at least 30 minutes before threading to prevent them from burning during cooking.

Teriyaki chicken skewers are a crowd-pleasing dish with a perfect balance of savory and sweet flavors. Whether served as an appetizer or a main course, they are sure to be a hit at your next meal or gathering.

Nut Butter Energy Bites

Ingredients:

- 1 cup rolled oats
- 1/2 cup nut butter (such as almond butter, peanut butter, or cashew butter)
- 1/3 cup honey or maple syrup
- 1/2 cup ground flaxseed or chia seeds
- 1 teaspoon vanilla extract
- 1/2 cup chocolate chips or chopped nuts (optional)
- A pinch of salt (optional)

Instructions:

Combine Ingredients:
- In a large bowl, mix together rolled oats, nut butter, honey or maple syrup, ground flaxseed or chia seeds, and vanilla extract. If desired, add a pinch of salt for flavor.

Add Optional Ingredients:
- Fold in chocolate chips or chopped nuts if you want to add extra texture and flavor to your energy bites.

Chill the Mixture:
- Place the mixture in the refrigerator for about 30 minutes. Chilling makes it easier to handle and shape into bites.

Shape into Bites:
- Once chilled, take small portions of the mixture and roll them between your hands to form bite-sized balls. Aim for a size that is easy to pop into your mouth.

Store or Enjoy:
- Place the energy bites on a plate or tray and refrigerate for an additional 15-20 minutes to firm up. Once firm, transfer them to an airtight container for storage.

Serve and Enjoy:
- Serve the nut butter energy bites as a quick snack or a pre-workout boost. They are also great for on-the-go energy.

Tips:

- Feel free to experiment with different nut butters and add-ins such as dried fruit, coconut flakes, or seeds for variety.

- Adjust the sweetness by adding more or less honey or maple syrup based on your preference.
- For a protein boost, consider adding a scoop of your favorite protein powder.

These nut butter energy bites are not only delicious but also packed with wholesome ingredients. They make for a satisfying and nutritious snack that can keep you fueled throughout the day.

Avocado Egg Rolls

Ingredients:

For the Egg Rolls:

- 2 ripe avocados, diced
- 1 cup red cabbage, shredded
- 1 carrot, julienned
- 1/4 cup red onion, finely chopped
- 2 tablespoons cilantro, chopped
- Juice of 1 lime
- Salt and pepper to taste
- Egg roll wrappers (square-shaped)
- Vegetable oil for frying

For Dipping Sauce:

- 1/4 cup soy sauce
- 2 tablespoons rice vinegar
- 1 tablespoon honey or maple syrup
- 1 teaspoon sesame oil
- 1 teaspoon grated ginger
- 1 clove garlic, minced
- Optional: Sriracha or chili flakes for heat

Instructions:

Prepare the Filling:
- In a bowl, combine diced avocados, shredded red cabbage, julienned carrot, chopped red onion, cilantro, lime juice, salt, and pepper. Mix well to create the filling.

Assemble the Egg Rolls:
- Lay an egg roll wrapper on a clean surface with one corner pointing toward you. Place a portion of the filling in the center of the wrapper.

Fold and Seal:
- Fold the bottom corner over the filling, then fold in the sides. Moisten the top corner with water and roll the wrapper tightly to seal the egg roll.

Repeat:
- Repeat the process with the remaining wrappers and filling.

Heat Oil:

- In a deep fryer or large skillet, heat vegetable oil to 350°F (180°C).

Fry the Egg Rolls:
- Carefully place the egg rolls in the hot oil, a few at a time, and fry until golden brown and crispy. This usually takes about 3-4 minutes. Use a slotted spoon to remove the egg rolls and place them on a paper towel-lined plate to absorb excess oil.

Prepare Dipping Sauce:
- In a small bowl, whisk together soy sauce, rice vinegar, honey or maple syrup, sesame oil, grated ginger, and minced garlic. Add Sriracha or chili flakes if you prefer a spicy kick.

Serve:
- Serve the avocado egg rolls warm with the dipping sauce on the side.

Tips:

- Ensure the avocado is ripe but firm for a creamy texture without being too mushy.
- Experiment with additional fillings such as bell peppers, jicama, or shredded chicken for variety.

These avocado egg rolls are a delightful fusion of creamy avocado and crunchy vegetables, wrapped in a crispy shell. They make for a crowd-pleasing appetizer or a tasty snack, especially when paired with the flavorful dipping sauce.

Beet Chips

Ingredients:

- 3-4 medium-sized beets, washed and peeled
- 2 tablespoons olive oil
- Salt and pepper to taste
- Optional: Dried herbs or spices (such as thyme, rosemary, or paprika)

Instructions:

Preheat the Oven:
- Preheat your oven to 350°F (175°C).

Slice the Beets:
- Using a mandoline slicer or a sharp knife, thinly slice the beets into uniform rounds. Aim for slices that are about 1/16 to 1/8 inch thick for consistent baking.

Toss with Olive Oil:
- In a large bowl, toss the beet slices with olive oil, ensuring each slice is lightly coated.

Season the Beet Chips:
- Sprinkle the beet slices with salt, pepper, and any optional dried herbs or spices. Toss again to evenly distribute the seasonings.

Arrange on Baking Sheets:
- Line baking sheets with parchment paper. Arrange the seasoned beet slices in a single layer, ensuring they are not overlapping. This allows for even baking.

Bake in the Oven:
- Bake in the preheated oven for 15-20 minutes, or until the edges of the beet chips begin to crisp up and turn slightly golden. Keep an eye on them to prevent burning.

Flip and Continue Baking:
- Carefully flip the beet chips using a spatula and continue baking for an additional 10-15 minutes or until they are crispy and fully dried.

Cool and Serve:
- Allow the beet chips to cool on the baking sheets. They will continue to crisp up as they cool. Once cooled, serve and enjoy!

Tips:

- Beets release natural sugars when baked, so a slight caramelization is normal and adds sweetness to the chips.
- Experiment with different seasonings to create unique flavor profiles.

These beet chips are not only visually appealing but also a nutritious snack. They are rich in antioxidants and provide a satisfying crunch. Enjoy them on their own or as a colorful addition to your favorite dips!

Raspberry Almond Brie Bites

Ingredients:

- Mini phyllo (filo) pastry shells (available in the frozen section)
- Brie cheese, cut into small cubes
- Raspberry jam
- Sliced almonds
- Fresh raspberries for garnish (optional)
- Honey for drizzling (optional)

Instructions:

Preheat the Oven:
- Preheat your oven according to the instructions on the phyllo pastry shell package.

Prepare the Phyllo Shells:
- Arrange the mini phyllo pastry shells on a baking sheet lined with parchment paper.

Add Brie Cubes:
- Place a small cube of brie cheese into each phyllo shell.

Top with Raspberry Jam:
- Add a small dollop of raspberry jam on top of each brie cube.

Sprinkle with Almonds:
- Sprinkle sliced almonds over the raspberry jam, adding a nice crunch to the bites.

Bake in the Oven:
- Bake in the preheated oven for the time specified on the phyllo pastry shell package or until the brie is melted and the edges of the pastry are golden brown.

Garnish and Drizzle (Optional):
- If desired, garnish the Raspberry Almond Brie Bites with fresh raspberries and drizzle a bit of honey over the top.

Serve Warm:
- Serve the bites warm, either on their own or as part of a cheese platter.

Tips:

- Adjust the sweetness by varying the amount of raspberry jam used.
- Consider adding a small fresh basil leaf on top for a burst of freshness.
- Experiment with different nuts or even a sprinkle of sea salt for added flavor.

These Raspberry Almond Brie Bites are a perfect combination of sweet and savory, making them a delightful addition to any party or gathering. The bite-sized portions make them easy to enjoy, and the contrasting textures create a mouthwatering experience.

Baked Buffalo Wings

Ingredients:

For the Wings:

- 2-3 pounds chicken wings, split into flats and drumettes
- 2 tablespoons baking powder (not baking soda)
- 1 teaspoon salt
- 1/2 teaspoon black pepper
- Optional: Celery sticks and carrot sticks for serving

For the Buffalo Sauce:

- 1/2 cup unsalted butter, melted
- 1/2 cup hot sauce (such as Frank's RedHot)
- 1/4 teaspoon garlic powder
- 1/4 teaspoon onion powder
- Optional: 1-2 tablespoons honey for a touch of sweetness

Instructions:

Preheat the Oven:
- Preheat your oven to 450°F (230°C).

Prepare the Wings:
- Pat the chicken wings dry with paper towels to remove excess moisture.

Coat with Baking Powder and Seasoning:
- In a bowl, toss the wings with baking powder, salt, and black pepper until the wings are evenly coated. The baking powder helps crisp up the skin during baking.

Arrange on Baking Sheets:
- Place a wire rack on each baking sheet. Arrange the seasoned wings on the racks in a single layer, ensuring they are not touching. This allows the hot air to circulate and crisp up the wings.

Bake in the Oven:
- Bake in the preheated oven for about 45-50 minutes or until the wings are golden brown and crispy.

Prepare the Buffalo Sauce:
- In a bowl, whisk together melted butter, hot sauce, garlic powder, onion powder, and honey if using.

Toss the Wings in Buffalo Sauce:

- Once the wings are out of the oven, transfer them to a large bowl. Pour the Buffalo sauce over the wings and toss until they are evenly coated.

Serve:
- Arrange the Baked Buffalo Wings on a serving platter and serve with celery and carrot sticks. You can also provide ranch or blue cheese dressing for dipping.

Tips:

- Adjust the level of heat by varying the amount of hot sauce in the Buffalo sauce.
- For extra crispiness, you can broil the wings for an additional 2-3 minutes after tossing them in the Buffalo sauce.

These Baked Buffalo Wings deliver the classic spicy and tangy flavor without the deep frying. They make for a great appetizer or game day snack that's sure to be a hit with friends and family.

Cottage Cheese and Pineapple Cups

Ingredients:

- Fresh pineapple, peeled, cored, and cut into small chunks
- Cottage cheese
- Honey or maple syrup for drizzling
- Optional: Chopped mint leaves for garnish

Instructions:

Prepare the Pineapple:
- Cut the fresh pineapple into small, bite-sized chunks. Ensure that the core is removed.

Assemble the Cups:
- In serving cups or bowls, layer a spoonful of cottage cheese with pineapple chunks.

Repeat Layers:
- Continue layering cottage cheese and pineapple until the cup is filled or to your desired proportions.

Drizzle with Honey or Maple Syrup:
- Drizzle honey or maple syrup over the cottage cheese and pineapple layers. Adjust the sweetness to your liking.

Garnish (Optional):
- Garnish the cups with chopped mint leaves for a burst of freshness.

Serve Chilled:
- Refrigerate the Cottage Cheese and Pineapple Cups for at least 30 minutes before serving. This allows the flavors to meld and the dish to chill.

Serve and Enjoy:
- Serve the cups chilled and enjoy the delightful combination of creamy cottage cheese with the sweet and juicy pineapple.

Tips:

- Consider adding a sprinkle of granola or chopped nuts for added texture.
- If using canned pineapple, choose pineapple chunks in juice rather than syrup for a healthier option.
- Customize the sweetness by adjusting the amount of honey or maple syrup.

Cottage Cheese and Pineapple Cups are a quick and nutritious snack, combining the creaminess of cottage cheese with the natural sweetness of pineapple. They are perfect for a light breakfast, afternoon snack, or a healthy dessert alternative.

Stuffed Dates with Goat Cheese

Ingredients:

- Medjool dates, pitted
- Goat cheese, softened
- Optional: Almonds or walnuts, whole or halved
- Honey for drizzling (optional)
- Fresh thyme leaves for garnish (optional)

Instructions:

Prepare the Dates:
- Using a small knife, make a lengthwise slit in each date to create an opening. Remove the pit, if not already done.

Stuff with Goat Cheese:
- Take a small amount of softened goat cheese and stuff it into the cavity of each date. You can use a spoon or your fingers to press the cheese into the date.

Optional Nut Filling:
- If desired, insert a whole or halved almond or walnut into the goat cheese-filled dates. This adds a crunchy texture.

Arrange on a Platter:
- Place the stuffed dates on a serving platter. Ensure they are arranged neatly and upright.

Drizzle with Honey (Optional):
- Drizzle honey over the stuffed dates for a touch of sweetness. This step is optional but adds extra flavor.

Garnish (Optional):
- Garnish with fresh thyme leaves for a herbal and aromatic element.

Serve:
- Serve the stuffed dates at room temperature and enjoy this delightful sweet and savory appetizer.

Tips:

- Adjust the amount of goat cheese based on personal preference.
- For a variation, you can sprinkle the stuffed dates with a pinch of sea salt for a contrast in flavors.

Stuffed dates with goat cheese are an elegant and easy-to-make appetizer that's perfect for entertaining or as a special treat. The combination of sweet dates and tangy goat cheese creates a harmonious blend of flavors that's sure to impress your guests.

Pretzel Bites with Mustard Dip

Ingredients:

For the Pretzel Bites:

- 1 1/2 cups warm water (110°F/43°C)
- 1 tablespoon sugar
- 2 teaspoons kosher salt
- 4 1/2 cups all-purpose flour
- 2 teaspoons active dry yeast
- 1/4 cup unsalted butter, melted
- Cooking spray or vegetable oil for greasing
- 10 cups water
- 2/3 cup baking soda
- 1 large egg yolk beaten with 1 tablespoon water (for egg wash)
- Pretzel salt or coarse sea salt for sprinkling

For the Mustard Dip:

- 1/2 cup Dijon mustard
- 2 tablespoons whole grain mustard
- 2 tablespoons honey
- 1 tablespoon mayonnaise

Instructions:

For the Pretzel Bites:

Activate Yeast:
- In a bowl, combine warm water, sugar, and kosher salt. Sprinkle the active dry yeast over the water mixture, and let it sit for about 5 minutes, or until it becomes foamy.

Mix Dough:
- In a large mixing bowl, combine the flour and melted butter. Pour in the yeast mixture and mix until the dough comes together.

Knead Dough:
- Turn the dough onto a floured surface and knead for about 5 minutes until it becomes smooth and elastic.

Let it Rise:

- Place the dough in a greased bowl, cover it with a clean kitchen towel, and let it rise in a warm place for about 1 hour or until it doubles in size.

Preheat Oven:
- Preheat your oven to 450°F (230°C). Line baking sheets with parchment paper.

Boil Pretzel Bites:
- Bring 10 cups of water and baking soda to a boil in a large pot. While waiting for it to boil, divide the dough into sections and roll each section into a long rope. Cut the ropes into bite-sized pieces.

Boil and Bake:
- Boil the pretzel bites in the baking soda water for about 30 seconds. Using a slotted spoon, transfer them to the prepared baking sheets. Brush the tops with egg wash and sprinkle with pretzel salt. Bake for 10-12 minutes or until golden brown.

For the Mustard Dip:
- In a small bowl, whisk together Dijon mustard, whole grain mustard, honey, and mayonnaise until well combined.

Serve:
- Serve the warm pretzel bites with the mustard dip on the side.

Tips:

- You can customize the mustard dip by adjusting the honey or adding a pinch of cayenne pepper for a spicy kick.
- Experiment with different types of mustard for unique flavors.

Enjoy these pretzel bites with mustard dip as a tasty snack or appetizer that's sure to be a hit at any gathering!

Chocolate Almond Clusters

Ingredients:

- 1 cup whole almonds
- 1 cup semi-sweet or dark chocolate chips
- 1 tablespoon coconut oil
- Sea salt (optional, for sprinkling)

Instructions:

Prepare a Baking Sheet:
- Line a baking sheet with parchment paper or a silicone baking mat.

Melt Chocolate:
- In a heatproof bowl, melt the chocolate chips and coconut oil together. You can do this using a double boiler or by microwaving in 20-second intervals, stirring between each interval until smooth.

Add Almonds:
- Stir in the whole almonds, making sure they are well-coated with the melted chocolate.

Form Clusters:
- Using a spoon or cookie scoop, drop small clusters of the chocolate-coated almonds onto the prepared baking sheet. You can shape them into clusters or leave them more rustic.

Set and Sprinkle (Optional):
- Allow the chocolate almond clusters to set at room temperature or, for faster setting, place them in the refrigerator for about 30 minutes. If desired, sprinkle a pinch of sea salt over the clusters before the chocolate sets.

Serve or Store:
- Once the clusters are set, remove them from the baking sheet and serve. If not serving immediately, store them in an airtight container at room temperature or in the refrigerator.

Tips:

- Experiment with different types of chocolate, such as milk chocolate or white chocolate, for variety.
- Customize the clusters by adding dried fruit, shredded coconut, or a sprinkle of your favorite spices.

These Chocolate Almond Clusters make for a delicious and satisfying treat. Whether enjoyed as a snack or presented as a homemade gift, they are sure to be a hit with chocolate and almond enthusiasts alike.

Smashed Avocado Toast

Ingredients:

- 1 ripe avocado
- 2 slices of your favorite bread (sourdough, whole grain, or multigrain work well)
- Salt and pepper to taste
- Optional toppings: cherry tomatoes, red pepper flakes, poached egg, feta cheese, or microgreens

Instructions:

Toast the Bread:
- Toast the slices of bread to your desired level of crispiness.

Smash the Avocado:
- While the bread is toasting, cut the ripe avocado in half, remove the pit, and scoop the flesh into a bowl. Use a fork to smash the avocado until it reaches your preferred level of smoothness or chunkiness.

Season the Avocado:
- Add salt and pepper to taste, and mix well to incorporate the seasoning into the smashed avocado.

Spread on Toast:
- Once the bread is toasted, spread the smashed avocado evenly over each slice.

Add Toppings (Optional):
- Customize your smashed avocado toast with additional toppings. Some popular choices include sliced cherry tomatoes, a sprinkle of red pepper flakes for a bit of heat, a poached egg for protein, crumbled feta cheese, or a handful of fresh microgreens.

Serve and Enjoy:
- Serve the smashed avocado toast immediately while the bread is still warm. It's a quick and tasty breakfast or snack option.

Tips:

- Drizzle a bit of olive oil or squeeze a touch of lemon juice over the smashed avocado for added flavor.
- Feel free to get creative with toppings based on your preferences and what you have on hand.

Smashed avocado toast is not only delicious but also a great way to enjoy the creamy texture and health benefits of avocados. It's a versatile dish that can be tailored to suit your taste and is perfect for any time of day.

Lemon Garlic Roasted Chickpeas

Ingredients:

- 2 cans (15 ounces each) chickpeas (garbanzo beans), drained and rinsed
- 2 tablespoons olive oil
- 2 cloves garlic, minced
- Zest of 1 lemon
- 1 tablespoon lemon juice
- 1 teaspoon dried thyme
- 1 teaspoon ground cumin
- 1/2 teaspoon paprika
- Salt and black pepper to taste

Instructions:

Preheat the Oven:
- Preheat your oven to 400°F (200°C).

Dry Chickpeas:
- Pat the drained chickpeas dry with a paper towel. Removing excess moisture helps achieve a crispier texture.

Season Chickpeas:
- In a bowl, combine the chickpeas with olive oil, minced garlic, lemon zest, lemon juice, dried thyme, ground cumin, paprika, salt, and black pepper. Toss well to coat the chickpeas evenly with the seasoning.

Spread on Baking Sheet:
- Spread the seasoned chickpeas in a single layer on a baking sheet lined with parchment paper. Ensure they are well-spaced for even roasting.

Roast in the Oven:
- Roast the chickpeas in the preheated oven for 25-30 minutes or until they are golden brown and crispy. Shake the pan or stir the chickpeas halfway through the roasting time for even cooking.

Cool and Serve:
- Allow the roasted chickpeas to cool slightly before serving. They will continue to crisp up as they cool.

Store:
- Store any leftovers in an airtight container at room temperature for up to a few days.

Tips:

- Experiment with additional spices like garlic powder, onion powder, or smoked paprika for different flavor variations.
- Feel free to adjust the level of lemon, garlic, and spices according to your taste preferences.

Lemon garlic roasted chickpeas make for a crunchy and satisfying snack that's perfect for munching on its own or adding to salads. They are a healthier alternative to traditional snacks and can be customized to suit your flavor preferences.

Pimento Cheese Stuffed Celery

Ingredients:

- 1 cup sharp cheddar cheese, shredded
- 1/2 cup cream cheese, softened
- 1/4 cup mayonnaise
- 1/4 cup diced pimentos, drained
- 1/4 teaspoon garlic powder
- 1/4 teaspoon onion powder
- Salt and black pepper to taste
- Celery stalks, washed and trimmed

Instructions:

Prepare the Pimento Cheese Filling:
- In a bowl, combine shredded sharp cheddar cheese, softened cream cheese, mayonnaise, diced pimentos, garlic powder, onion powder, salt, and black pepper. Mix well until all ingredients are thoroughly combined.

Clean and Trim Celery:
- Wash the celery stalks and trim off the ends. Cut the celery stalks into manageable lengths, about 3-4 inches long.

Fill Celery with Pimento Cheese:
- Using a small spoon or a piping bag, fill the hollow part of each celery stalk with the pimento cheese mixture. Smooth the filling for a neat presentation.

Serve:
- Arrange the pimento cheese stuffed celery on a serving platter.

Chill (Optional):
- If you prefer a chilled appetizer, you can refrigerate the stuffed celery for about 30 minutes before serving.

Garnish (Optional):
- Garnish with additional diced pimentos, chopped chives, or a sprinkle of paprika for added color and flavor.

Serve and Enjoy:
- Serve the pimento cheese stuffed celery as a tasty and satisfying appetizer for gatherings or as a snack.

Tips:

- Customize the pimento cheese filling by adding ingredients like hot sauce, Worcestershire sauce, or a dash of cayenne pepper for extra kick.
- Make the pimento cheese filling ahead of time and refrigerate until ready to use.

Pimento cheese stuffed celery is a timeless and crowd-pleasing appetizer, perfect for parties, picnics, or any occasion where you want a delicious and easy-to-eat snack.

www.ingramcontent.com/pod-product-compliance
Lightning Source LLC
LaVergne TN
LVHW081604060526
838201LV00054B/2080